1 MONTH OF
FREE
READING

at
www.ForgottenBooks.com

By purchasing this book you are eligible for one month membership to ForgottenBooks.com, giving you unlimited access to our entire collection of over 1,000,000 titles via our web site and mobile apps.

To claim your free month visit:

www.forgottenbooks.com/free893017

ISBN 978-0-265-81093-4
PIBN 10893017

MH88D0154

United States
Department of
Agriculture

FNS–250

United States
Department of
Health and
Human Services

Cross-Cultural
Counseling
A Guide for
Nutrition and
Health Counselors

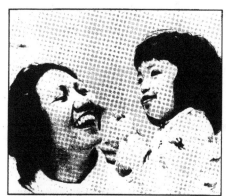

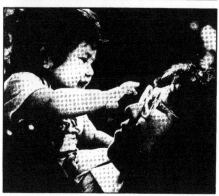

Preface

The U.S. Department of Agriculture (USDA)/Department of Health and Human Services (DHHS) Nutrition Education Committee for Maternal and Child Nutrition Publications was formally established in 1980. Its purpose is to promote a joint effort between the USDA and the DHHS on education materials related to maternal and child nutrition in order to assure consistency of content, avoid duplication, and make more effective use of resources. By providing a systematic mechanism for representatives of various agencies within USDA and DHHS to exchange information on nutrition education, this committee has stimulated greater collaboration on joint projects. This publication is one example.

The Maternal and Child Health Program of DHHS, and the Special Supplemental Food Program for Women, Infants, and Children and the Commodity Supplemental Food Program of USDA, provide services aimed at improving the nutrition and health status of women, infants, and children from diverse cultural, religious, and ethnic groups. The USDA/DHHS committee identified a mutual need for information on cultural considerations in counseling. In response to this need, *Cross-Cultural Counseling: A Guide for Nutrition and Health Counselors* was developed collaboratively to assist program staff in providing culturally appropriate counseling to the special population groups served by USDA and DHHS programs. While many of the examples in this guide relate to mothers and children, the principles are applicable to all persons at any age.

We are interested in your response to this publication. After reading it, will you please take a few minutes to complete the questionnaire on the back page?

CONTENTS

September 1986

Acknowledgments

The following persons had major responsibility for preparing this publication:

Technical Content:

Brenda Schilling, M.S., R.D.
Nutrition and Technical Services Division
Food and Nutrition Service
U.S. Department of Agriculture

Elizabeth Brannon, M.S., R.D.
Division of Maternal and Child Health
Public Health Service
U.S. Department of Health and Human Services

Editorial Assistance:

Christopher Kocsis, Public Information, USDA

Format and Word Processing

Monica Shields

We would like to acknowledge and express our appreciation to the following individuals who assisted in developing and reviewing this publication:

Marsha Hardin, Director
Community Outreach Programs
La Leche International

Robert Kohls, Executive Director
Washington International Center

Lilia Parekh, Nutritionist
Children's Hospital
National Medical Center

Margaret Range, Consultant
School For International Living

Tony Whitehead, Ph.D.
Department of Health Education
University of North Carolina

Catherine Wong, Nutritionist
District Health Center No. 4
San Francisco Department of Public Health

Members of the USDA/DHHS Nutrition
Education Committee for Maternal
and Child Nutrition Publications

Introduction

The United States is a land of people with diverse cultural and ethnic backgrounds, whether newly arrived immigrants or American cultural minorities. As a counselor you are faced with the challenge of providing education and assistance to people with cultures that may be quite different from your own. How well can you meet the challenge?

There will probably be a time when every counselor is called on to serve clients from a culture different from his or her own. The purpose of this guide is to increase awareness of, and provide information for counseling clients with, different beliefs, customs, and behaviors related to food and health. A "standard" approach to counseling that does not consider a client's cultural background can create barriers that block effective communication. To get your message across to the client requires culturally appropriate communication strategies.

Culture can be viewed as a set of beliefs, assumptions, and values, widely shared by a group, that structures behavior of group members from birth until death. There are variations within each cultural group due to differences in socioeconomic status, social class, religion, age, education, location, and length of time in the United States. However, people from a given culture will tend to have experiences that are culturally patterned and similar in nature, although not identical.

We will use generalizations about cultural groups to illustrate the importance of cultural sensitivity in counseling clients. The examples are not intended to stereotype or to imply that all people from the same cultural group are identical or approachable in exactly the same manner. You should use these generalizations only as a means to stimulate your awareness of cultural differences, and to form some basic hypotheses about the cultural groups you may be serving.

This guide is not intended to give you indepth information about specific cultural groups. Rather, it is designed to help you as a counselor to develop a greater awareness of the problems in cross-cultural counseling and how to approach those problems. While you do not need to know all there is to know about another culture, it is advisable to acquire basic knowledge of the cultural groups with whom you work routinely.

Even more important than the knowledge, though, are awareness, respect, and acceptance of the client's cultural beliefs and practices as equally valid as your own. Many of the considerations discussed are just a part of good counseling in general, but are emphasized in this guide because of their importance in cross-cultural counseling. This guide can help you develop the understanding, acceptance, and skill necessary for effective cross-cultural counseling.

The Selected Bibliography includes references on cross-cultural communication, cultural influences on health and nutrition, and considerations for working with specific cultural groups. The Appendix provides additional information on sociocultural and dietary practices of selected cultural groups.

Keys to Counseling

Understanding

One key to cross-cultural counseling is an understanding of value systems in other cultures and their influence on health and nutrition. Every culture has a value system that dictates behavior directly or indirectly in that it sets norms and teaches that those norms are right. Health and nutrition beliefs and practices, in particular, reflect that value system.

Cultural Values

A value is a standard that people use to assess themselves and others. It is a widely held belief about what is worthwhile, desirable, or important for well-being. Counseling clients from diverse backgrounds requires understanding your own values as well as the values of other groups. Too often we interpret the behaviors of others as being negative or inferior because we do not understand the underlying value system of their culture. Values that one culture views as positive may be considered undesirable or threatening in another. It is important to realize that values commonly found in the United States may be repulsive to some other cultures. Simply exposing clients to a new idea or practice will not automatically result in adoption if that idea or practice conflicts with their values.

There is a natural tendency for people to be "culture bound," to assume that their values, customs, and behaviors are admirable, sensible, and right. Cross-cultural counseling presents a special challenge because it requires you to work with clients without making judgments as to the superiority of one set of values over another. To enhance your understanding of cultural differences in values the following list provides a general comparison of dominant Anglo-American values with values commonly found in some other more tradition-bound countries (1).*

Common Values

Some Other Cultures' Values	Anglo-American Values
Fate	Personal Control Over the Environment
Tradition	Change
Human Interaction Dominates	Time Dominates
Hierarchy/Rank/Status	Human Equality
Group Welfare	Individualism/Privacy
Birthright Inheritance	Self-Help
Cooperation	Competition
Past Orientation	Future Orientation
"Being" Orientation	Action/Goal/Work Orientation
Formality	Informality
Indirectness/Ritual/"Face"	Directness/Openness/Honesty
Idealism/Theory	Practicality/Efficiency
Spiritualism/Detachment	Materialism

*Numbers in parentheses correspond to references listed on page 21.

Examples of Potential Differences in Values

- Clients and counselors may differ on the value of time. Most of us are ruled by time and schedules. If "being on time" and "not wasting time" are not familiar concepts to the client, a 10 o'clock appointment may not be kept until 11 or 12 o'clock and the client will consider this entirely appropriate behavior.

- The idea of receiving food that should not be shared with other family members, but must be consumed by the client alone, may be incomprehensible if the client is from a culture where the group's welfare is always placed before the individual's.

- A client may not follow the dietary practices you suggest because of extended family values and practices. Decisions regarding food intake might not be decided by that individual, but by group or family consensus.

- A client may not understand that his/her health habits are related to well-being, but will rather attribute ill health to "God's will." Thus, prevention may be viewed as a useless attempt to control one's fate.

Health Beliefs

Cultures vary in their beliefs of the cause, prevention, and treatment of illness. These beliefs dictate the practices used to maintain health. Health practices can be classified as 1) folk practices, 2) spiritual or psychic healing practices, and 3) conventional medical practices (2). Some cultures closely tie religious beliefs to state of health. When illness is viewed as a curse for sins, people may seek a cure through good deeds and forgiveness from a spiritual source rather than through medical care. For instance, in some Black communities "laying on of hands" and prayer are used as common methods of healing (3).

The value placed on "good health" is also variable. The Anglo-American culture emphasizes *duration* in life, whereas some other cultures place greater emphasis

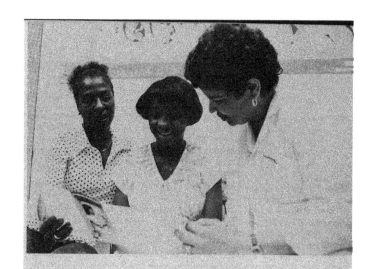

on the *quality* of life. From culture to culture, the perception of health will differ. Anglo-Americans believe thinness to be a desirable health goal, whereas other groups such as Haitians may consider thin people to be in poor health and fat people to be healthy and happy (4). Similarly, cleanliness is not closely associated with good health in some cultures. Natural body odors are acceptable and desirable, rather than offensive, in many cultures. Adoption of hygienic practices that have a positive effect on health, such as brushing the teeth, may need to be explained and promoted with clients.

Cultures do not uniformly categorize conditions as diseases or illnesses. A condition considered normal in one culture may be defined as a disease in another. For example, tuberculosis may be so common in a given culture that its symptoms are viewed as normal. Also, when no acute symptoms are present clients may be unwilling to seek health care. Children may not be brought in for care when they have skin eruptions or ear infections because the parents do not consider them ill (5). Preventive health checkups, such as dental or eye exams, may be avoided or considered unnecessary because no symptoms are present. Prenatal care may be delayed or avoided because child-bearing is seen as a natural and personal process. For employed clients, seeking health care may mean time away from their jobs and lost income. For some cultures, such as Hispanic, it may also signify a lack of strength and control over their lives (5).

Your clients may follow a specific process in seeking health care. They seek advice from family in choosing a healer or a course of treatment. Cultural healers often may be used instead of conventional medical care. For example, in some Black communities cultural healers, who are highly respected and valued, provide both physical and emotional support to clients who believe in them (3). The family supports and also frequently is involved in the treatment and cure. Western medicine too often makes the mistake of cutting off that support system by dealing with the client alone (2). Clients may need to consult with the support system before making a medical decision. Unconventional beliefs and practices must be respected. Many have survived for generations and are in fact effective. You need to work with the client to develop an acceptable plan which builds on his or her beliefs in a positive way and involves the support group.

Health-Related Dietary Practices

Diet is commonly used by many cultures to both prevent and treat an illness. For Anglo-Americans nutrition has become extremely important as a preventive measure for almost all diseases. Among some other cultures common practices to prevent and cure diseases involve the balancing of body fluids, or "humors," between hot and cold. These practices stem from the Greek theory of disease that considers illness to be the result of humoral imbalance causing the body to become too hot or too cold (6).

Particularly, Asian and Hispanic cultures subscribe to a "hot-cold theory" of health and diet. The "hot-cold theory" describes intrinsic properties of a food, beverage, or medicine and its effect on the body. It is not necessarily related to the spiciness or temperature of the substance.

The classification of foods, beverages, and medicines as "hot" or "cold" varies within each cultural group. In general, warm or hot foods are believed to be easier to digest than cold or cool foods. Illnesses are treated with substances having the opposite property of the illness in order to achieve balance. Conditions thought to be caused by exposure to cold or chilling are cured by "hot" medicines as well as by ingesting "hot" foods and beverages. The reverse is true of illnesses brought about by exposure to heat. The following table by Harwood illustrates the hot-cold classification among Puerto Ricans (7).

The Hot-Cold Classification Among Puerto Ricans

	Frio (cold)	Fresco (cool)	Caliente (hot)
Illnesses or bodily conditions	Arthritis Menstrual period Pain in the joints	Colds	Constipation Diarrhea Pregnancy Rashes Ulcers
Medicine and herbs		Bicarbonate of soda Linden flowers Milk of magnesia Nightshade Orange flower water Sage Tobacco	Anise Aspirin Castor oil Cinnamon Cod liver oil Iron tablets Penicillin Vitamins
Foods	Avocado Banana Coconut Lima beans Sugar cane White beans	Barley water Whole milk Chicken Fruits Honey Raisins Salt cod Watercress Onions Peas	Alcoholic beverages Chili peppers Chocolate Coffee Corn meal Evaporated milk Garlic Kidney beans

Asians, such as Indochinese, may believe in the "Yin" and "Yang" forces and their influence on health. "Yin" represents female, cold, and darkness, while "Yang" represents male, hot, and light (8). When foods are digested they turn into air which is either "Yin" or "Yang." Excesses of one force are treated with foods from the opposite force to achieve a balance. "Cold" (Yin) foods include most fruits and vegetables, seaweed, bean sprouts, cold drinks, juices, and rice water; "hot" (Yang) foods include ginger, chicken, meat, pig's feet, meat broth, nuts, fried food, coffee, spices, and infant formula (8).

Maternal Health

As previously mentioned, women from other cultures may not seek early prenatal care because pregnancy is not considered a condition requiring medical attention. Fear, modesty, or cultural taboos may also cause some women to avoid health examinations by a male physician. In cultures where home delivery is the norm, clients may resist going to a hospital for delivery.

Folk medicine related to pregnancy is a common practice among people of many cultures, including some Anglo-Americans. This often relates to the belief that the fetus can be affected both positively and negatively by maternal experiences, emotions, exposures, and eating habits during pregnancy. Certain foods are believed to promote a healthy baby, while other foods are feared to deform or damage the fetus, cause a miscarriage, or make delivery difficult. An example is the belief that not satisfying a food craving or overindulging in a food can cause a birthmark resembling the craved food or an allergy to that food in the infant (9). For instance, an unsatisfied craving for strawberries or cherries may be thought to cause red birthmarks, whereas a chocolate craving may be considered a cause of brown marks (9). Therefore, it becomes not just acceptable, but necessary, for pregnant women holding such beliefs to satisfy their cravings.

Some pregnant women crave nonfood items such as laundry starch, clay, or ice. Starch eating is more frequently reported among Black women, while clay eating is reported among the other cultural groups including Hispanics as well as Blacks (9). The consumption of nonfood items is called pica. The reasons for pica are not clear; however, several theories have been suggested for pica including the body's need to acquire certain nutrients, hunger, cultural tradition, prevention of nausea, and attention seeking (2). Regardless of the reason for pica, it is important to determine if clients practice it and to what degree. Large amounts of nonfood substances are likely to replace nutritious foods needed by a pregnant woman. Clay can bind nutrients, particularly iron, and prevent their absorption. Also, clay consumed in large quantities can obstruct the gastrointestinal tract. Fortunately, most women who practice pica do so on a limited basis (6). If the extent is very limited, and the woman is able to consume an adequate diet, intervention may not be necessary.

Western medicine now recognizes the importance of adequate weight gain during pregnancy to produce larger and healthier infants. Some cultures believe that weight gain must be restricted to produce a small infant and an easy delivery. This belief may be related to the level of obstetric care that was available to women in their native country. A large baby can pose a serious threat to a pregnant woman with a small pelvis when adequate medical care is not available during delivery.

Hot-cold theories of disease and health have an influence on practices in both the prenatal and postpartum periods. The third trimester of pregnancy is generally regarded as "hot" (7). A client might avoid hot foods and medications, such as iron supplements, during this period. In contrast, cold foods might be avoided for 1 or 2 months after delivery because cold foods are believed to slow the flow of blood and prevent the emptying of the uterus (7). For example, some Asian women may abstain from vegetables, fruits, and fruit juices for 30 days postpartum because those foods are considered too cold and could endanger their health (8).

Child Health

Infant feeding practices are culturally determined. Although breastfeeding is the usual method in non-Western countries, those same cultures may not choose breastfeeding once they are in the United States. Middle- and upper-class Anglo-American women are more likely to breastfeed than other cultural groups. In contrast, Black Americans have the lowest rate of breastfeeding (10). However, the subcultures within each group will vary in the extent to which they choose breastfeeding. For example, Puerto Ricans may choose breastfeeding more often than Cubans (10). In general, cultural values influence women's perceptions about breastfeeding in terms of nutritional value, the father's feelings, breast exposure, sexuality, and convenience. Also, breastfeeding may often be viewed as less modern and prestigious than bottle feeding.

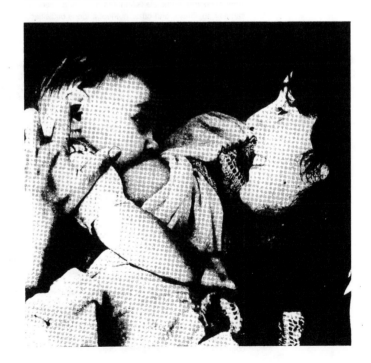

Folk medicine influences breastfeeding. In some Hispanic and Asian groups breastfeeding is delayed for several days after birth because colostrum is considered dirty and not acceptable for infants (8, 11). In addition, Hispanic women often believe that stress and anger in the mother will produce "bad milk" and make the infant ill (10). Women with a tendency toward a bad temper may think it is unwise to breastfeed.

Introduction of solid foods is frequently associated with some aspect of the infant's development. In Western medicine, it relates to when an infant can hold up his or her head and sit with support. In other cultures, it may relate to the eruption of the first tooth, the reaching out for adult foods, or the cessation of breastfeeding. Often cultures judge a mother by how much her infant eats and how quickly the infant gains weight. Consequently, an obese infant may be desired because it reflects good health and good care. However, in some Asian cultures it is not uncommon for a 16-month-old child to be fed entirely on milk without any solid foods (8). Sometimes rice water, which is low in calories and iron, is added at 6-8 months of age. This practice can lead to failure to thrive.

Hot-cold classifications also apply to the health of infants and children. Rashes, diarrhea, fever, and many other childhood diseases are classified as "hot" and, therefore, require cool or cold medications and fluids. Hispanics may switch infants from canned formula, classified as "hot," to a "cool" food such as whole milk to remedy an illness, and other nutritious foods classified as "hot" may be restricted in the diet (7). Likewise, in some Asian cultures, rice water, fruit juices, and sugar water may be fed to an infant to counteract the "hot" formula (8).

Approaches to Dietary Change

Helping people improve their nutrition practices first requires an understanding of and appreciation for their culture and its practices. Eating is a personal matter carrying with it great cultural significance. Thus, people tend to change more conspicuous aspects of their cultural background such as clothing and language first, and food habits last. In providing nutrition counseling, you must take into consideration the symbolism of food, such as the meaning of soul food to Black Americans, which grew out of the necessity of surviving as slaves and out of a need to express the group feeling of "soul."

People never eat all that is edible in their environment. Culture will determine what are acceptable and unacceptable foods. When counseling a client, try to categorize nutrition practices as beneficial, neutral, or harmful. You will want to promote change only in those practices that are harmful to the client. Beneficial or neutral practices should be supported and encouraged regardless of the reason and even when contrary to your own practices. You should bear in mind that many common American practices seem strange or illogical to persons from other cultures. What could be more unusual than the person who boils water to make tea, adds ice to make it cold again, adds sugar to sweeten it, and then adds lemon to sour it?

If your clients are recent immigrants you may need to help them first with basic survival skills such as buying, storing, and preparing the foods found in their new environment. Clients' foods habits and beliefs should always be the basis on which to build or improve dietary practices. For example, if you want to encourage fluid intake with a Hispanic client you might suggest drinking more herbal tea, a common beverage among those cultures (6). You will want to assure clients that

Anglo-American foods are not necessarily better choices than their own culture's food choices. Likewise, the standard approach of "the basic four food groups and three meals a day" should not be emphasized if it conflicts with the client's cultural dietary patterns. Remember to ask the client about possible food restrictions, taboos, or intolerances so that acceptable alternatives can be found without compromising nutrient intake.

In suggesting dietary changes, you should be aware that most people of other than northern European descent may have some degree of intolerance to the milk sugar, lactose. In fact, two-thirds of the world's population experiences lactose intolerance after early childhood due to reduced production of the enzyme lactase (6). The majority of American Blacks, Asians, Native Americans, Hispanics, and Middle Easterners are lactose deficient to some degree. In those groups, symptoms after drinking milk may include gas, intestinal pain, cramps, and possibly vomiting or diarrhea. You are likely to find many non-Anglo-American clients avoiding milk because of the discomfort it causes. Thus, it will be necessary to find other culturally appropriate sources of calcium for those clients. For example, you might suggest leafy green vegetables, bok choy, tofu (soybean curd), and fish with edible bones as calcium sources for Asians. For Hispanics, you could encourage the consumption of corn tortillas (if the corn they were made from has been treated with lime—calcium carbonate), cheese, and cafe con leche (coffee with milk). For any client with lactose intolerance, you might also suggest fermented milk products such as yogurt, lactose-reduced milks, and sweet acidophilus milk to provide calcium.

9

Intertwined with cultural food practices are religious dietary regulations. Almost all religions use foods as symbols in celebrations and rituals. Many food taboos and restrictions relate to religious beliefs, such as the avoidance of pork by Black Muslims or the forbiddance of beef to Hindus. Knowing the client's religious practices related to food allows you to suggest improvements or modifications that will not conflict with dietary laws.

Some cultures prefer to have social contacts only with their extended family and not with strangers; therefore, group nutrition education activities may not be appropriate for them (11). You may find individual client contacts to be more effective for cross-cultural counseling, particularly when the family's decision-maker, if other than the client, is included in the discussion.

For many ethnic groups, particulary recent immigrants, respect for authority and politeness in public may prevent a client from raising questions about your recommendations. You may need to ask several times if there are any questions or any objections to your recommendations. You may even want to point out that other alternatives are possible if they are unable to follow your recommendations.

It is sometimes a difficult task in cross-cultural counseling to determine how well the message is understood by the client. Asking the client directly or through an interpreter to repeat the instructions, demonstrate the procedures, or summarize the main points of discussion will help provide feedback as to the success of communication efforts (12). Limiting discussion to the most relevant and understandable information and using culturally appropriate methods will help you get the message across. Teaching one concept at a time can help prevent the client from being overwhelmed with information.

The degree of compliance in cross-cultural counseling may be less than you expect. If a client's values are inconsistent with the underlying rationale for recommended change, the probability of noncompliance is high. Clients may agree to do something out of courtesy or fear, but may have no intention of following through with your recommendations. Limited understanding of health issues may act as a disincentive for client compliance, particularly for preventive measures when there are no signs or symptoms to relieve. Compliance that involves spending money will require an even higher level of commitment, particularly from low-income clients.

Having realistic expectations will give you a sense of accomplishment and help you avoid frustration. Knowledge that a practice is harmful does not necessarily promote change in that behavior, as is commonly seen in people who smoke. This is true regardless of the client's cultural background. You should not feel solely responsible for a client's health. You must balance the client's right to determine his or her own future against your need as a counselor to promote change. The goal should be to provide counseling in a positive and culturally appropriate manner, which encourages learning and promotes behavioral change. The rest is up to the client.

Communicating

Counseling can be effective only if both you and the client perceive the communication process to be possible and profitable. Communication involves not only what you say and how you say it, but also what you imply and what your listener perceives. It is the other key to successful cross-cultural counseling.

The Counselor

Your personality and communicating style affect the counseling process. Your clients may easily detect attitudes you think you are concealing. Some minority groups, such as Black Americans, have been taught to observe and listen carefully for implications of racism (3). Genuine interest in and concern for the client are essential qualities for the cross-cultural counselor. Insincerity, bias, and prejudice will negate your counseling efforts.

When small groups migrate into a larger society, they are frequently termed "ethnic groups." Ethnicity usually reflects affiliation with a national or racial heritage. Ideally, the ethnic background of the counselor should be the same as that of the client. However, in most situations it is not feasible to have a counselor for each cultural group served. Understanding and respect for all cultures can help to overcome many of the differences between you and the client. Frequently, you will receive respect from clients regardless of culture simply because you are a professional. When peer counselors are used, people with backgrounds similar to those of your clients are the best choices. However, you must also guard against assumptions that, for example, one Southeast Asian can easily counsel another. Variables such as socioeconomic status can alter how people from a given culture interact.

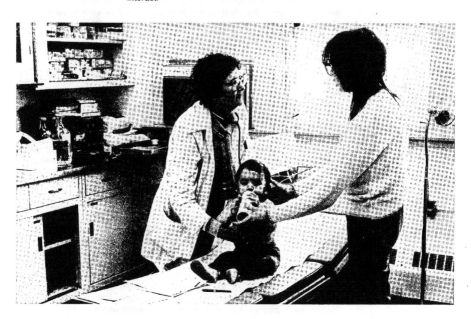

Nonverbal Communication

Messages are communicated by facial expressions and body movements which are specific to each culture. You should be aware of variations in nonverbal communication to avoid misunderstandings or inappropriate movements which may unintentionally offend clients. Also, you should use caution in interpreting the client's facial expressions or body movements. Your interpretation might be quite different from the client's intent.

Silence

You may view silence as awkward or wasteful of time. However, some cultures are quite comfortable with periods of silence. Clients who view silence as a normal part of a conversation may not appreciate your efforts to fill the void with "small talk." Some Native Americans, for example, consider a minute and a half to be a normal amount of time to wait to respond, while Arab friends may spend 30 minutes or more sitting together in silence (13). Conversely, some cultures consider it entirely appropriate to speak before the other person has finished talking; therefore, you should avoid mistaking this overlap as rude behavior on the part of the client. Being tolerant of natural pauses or interruptions in the communication process will help foster the client's respect.

Distance

The most comfortable physical distance between you and another person varies from culture to culture. The Anglo-American generally prefers to be about an arm's length distance away from another person (5). Hispanics usually prefer closer proximity than Anglo-Americans, in contrast to Asians, who tend to prefer greater distance (14). Giving the client options for space preference, such as saying, "Please have a seat wherever you like," can help you establish the proper distance for that client.

Eye Contact

The amount of eye contact that is comfortable varies with each culture. Many Anglo-Americans are brought up to look people straight in the eye. However, older Black Americans may have been taught not to make eye contact with whites (15). Staring is considered impolite by some groups, including Native Americans and Asians (3, 16). However, if you avoid eye contact or break eye contact too frequently, as you might to complete paper work, it may be misinterpreted by the client as disinterest. Observing the client both when listening and speaking can offer clues to appropriate eye contact. Also, you can arrange seating to meet the situation such as by sitting next to the client, rather than across from him or her, to reduce direct eye contact.

Emotional Expression

Expression of emotion between people of different cultures varies from very expressive, as with Hispanics, to total nonexpressiveness, as with Asians (5). We have a tendency to regard people who are more expressive as immature and those who are less expressive as unfeeling (5). Happiness and sorrow are emotions common to all people, but they may not be openly expressed, particularly to outsiders. Varying beliefs about the origin and treatment of pain will dictate different emotional behaviors in different cultures. Also, some cultures, such as Asian, may smile or laugh to mask other emotions (5).

Body Language

The position, gestures, and motion of the body can be interpreted differently depending on the culture. The use of hands is a common vehicle for nonverbal expression. A firm handshake may be a positive gesture of goodwill in the dominant Anglo-American culture, but some other cultures prefer only a light touch. For instance, a vigorous handshake may be viewed as a sign of aggression by some Native Americans (16). Touching or being touched by a stranger may be considered inappropriate or an intimacy signal, as is the case with many Asians, but entirely appropriate with many Hispanics (5,15). Standing with hands on hips may imply anger to some clients. Pointing or beckoning with a finger may appear disrespectful, particularly to Asians who use that gesture to call their dogs (3). Positioning of feet also can be misinterpreted. Pointing a foot toward someone or showing the bottom part of a shoe is considered disrespectful by Asian clients (3). Conservative use of body language is prudent when you are uncertain as to what is appropriate within a cultural group. Observing the client's actions and interactions with others may give you direction for acceptable body language. Being open with clients and asking general questions about body language can also help if you have doubts about appropriate behavior.

Verbal Communication

How you speak is as important as what you say in cross-cultural counseling. Your tone of voice should be positive, avoiding a condescending, disinterested, or unpleasant tone. The volume should be audible, but not so loud as to make your client feel uncomfortable. Often we mistakenly assume that a louder voice is clearer and therefore better understood by the client. Articulation of each word is important, especially for the client whose native language is not English. You may

even have to adjust speech rate. Speech that is too rapid might not be understood, while speech that is too slow might actually bore the client. Clients who speak slowly may not need to be spoken to at that rate. You might ask "Am I speaking too fast?" and adjust your rate appropriately. Avoiding slang and technical jargon will also help your client understand.

You should not try to imitate an ethnic communication style which is not naturally your own. For example, using Black American language and communication style, when you are not of Black American heritage, may be misinterpreted as ridicule (3).

Formality

Anglo-Americans tend to be informal in their verbal communication, but some other cultures prefer to keep a relationship more formal. You should not assume that a first-name basis is appropriate for client relationships. Many Black Americans may view being addressed by a first name as too familiar and may infer disrespect (3). In Vietnamese and Chinese cultures people have three- or four-word names. The first word is the family name, the second word the middle name, and the last one or two words the given name. The given name is usually preferred along with the title of Mr. or Mrs. (17). With any client, terms of endearment such as "honey," or potentially derogatory terms such as "boy" or "girl" when referring to adults, should be avoided. Asking the client how he or she prefers to be addressed is the easiest solution, or assume formality when in doubt.

Rapport

Establishing rapport with your client is important when beginning the counseling session. You should use "small talk" to reflect genuine concern for the client. Too much chatting, too many questions, or being "too nice" may cause uneasiness or raise suspicion. An opening question such as "How may I help you?" can provide an opportunity for clients to express their problems. If a client is not responsive to an open-ended question, you might suggest several options for the client to choose from. Silence on the part of the client does not necessarily reflect disinterest, but rather may be a thoughtful reaction to a question. Demonstrating patience, respect, and awareness of the client's culture can greatly help to establish rapport.

Subject

The subject matter may influence the success of counseling. Certain subjects may not be acceptable for discussion. For example, clients may be unwilling to discuss personal or family affairs with an unfamiliar counselor because those matters are considered to be private. Also, asking about family or spouses is not considered appropriate in every culture (16). Religious beliefs may be a taboo subject; therefore, actions based on them may be sensitive or difficult to discuss. You may be able to phrase questions in ways that are culturally more appropriate and explain why it is necessary to ask certain questions. You can also say to the client, "Please tell me if you do not want to answer."

Within the image: Milk / Leche · Fruits & Vegetables / Frutas y Vegetales · Protein / Proteina · Breads & Cereals · Other Foods / Otros Alimentos · Nutrients · Protein / Proteina · Calcium / Calcio · Iron / Hierro · Vitamin C / Vitamina C

Overcoming the Language Barrier

English as a Second Language

If you have ever tried to master a foreign language, you can appreciate the problems facing the client for whom English is a second language. He or she may have difficulty expressing throughts and concerns in English, and will require more of your time and patience.

You will want to allow sufficient time for the client to formulate answers to questions. Use simple vocabulary, and speak slowly and clearly; try to find words the client understands. Repeating the same words in a louder voice will not increase comprehension unless the client is hard of hearing; becoming frustrated with yourself or the client will only aggravate the situation. Furthermore, a loud voice may be interpreted as hostility or disrespect. Ignoring the client, or halting the conversation and turning to another activity, such as paperwork, are unproductive and will only serve to increase the client's feeling of isolation.

Generally, your client will understand English better than he or she speaks it because of the difficulty in finding the right words. Remember that fluency in spoken or written English does not correlate with intelligence. Also, some clients may not be able to read their native language. Some clients will be able to speak, but not read, English well—or vice versa. Do not automatically assume that the level of fluency in speaking reflects the appropriate reading level when you are choosing written materials, whether in English or translated. It is wise to check for comprehension before distributing written materials to clients with questionable reading skills. For clients who do not read in any language, try using materials such as pictures, food models, and actual packages.

The Non-English-Speaking Client

If you and the client do not speak the same language direct communication may be difficult or impossible. In that case, an interpreter must be included in the counseling process. Concepts which are foreign to either you or the client can be explained by the interpreter. Also, an interpreter may be able to establish rapport with the client, thus eliciting more information.

There are, however, limitations and drawbacks in using interpreters. It adds another step and, therefore, additional time in the counseling process. In general, translations tend to be simplistic, not reflecting the nonverbal and emotional expression. Some words or concepts may be difficult to translate due to a lack of vocabulary or to the personal nature of the subject matter. For example, in Cambodia there is no direct translation for the word anemia, so the word must be explained to clients (8). You should be aware that interpreters may censor or translate information from the client into what they think you want to hear.

When interpreters are necessary, they should be carefully selected. Bilingual staff and community volunteers can be used when hiring qualified interpreters is not feasible. Adult family members or friends of the client are also possible choices. Children, however, should not be asked to translate because of the value many cultures place on adults as authority figures and the possible inappropriateness of some subject matter for children. Enlisting interpreters from the waiting room is not recommended because some ethnic groups, such as Puerto Ricans, consider it a breach of confidentiality to have a stranger interpret for them (4). Also, you should not assume that any Latin or Asian can interpret for all others of the same cultural root. Puerto Ricans and Mexicans do not speak identical languages nor do Cambodians and Vietnamese. Mistaking one group for another may offend clients because they take pride in their ethnic origin.

You can do several things to improve the interpretation process. To begin, you should instruct the interpreter on the goals of the program and the purpose of the counseling. Then, to enhance nonverbal communication, seat the interpreter so as not to obstruct your visual contact with the client. Also, try addressing your client directly instead of directing your statements to the interpreter. You will want to avoid slang words, complex ideas, difficult abstractions, or lengthy speeches without pauses. Instead, use language and examples your interpreter can understand and translate. Instruct interpreters to use the client's own words instead of paraphrasing, and encourage them to ask for further explanation whenever a word or phrase is unclear.

Acquiring Accurate Information

All counselors are concerned about getting accurate information from clients, and this intensifies when the counseling is cross-cultural. Finding approaches that yield true information is easier once you are aware of some additional barriers to communication.

Possible Barriers

There are several reasons why a client may not provide you with correct information. Clients may not trust you because you are a stranger or you resemble in appearance or position someone with whom they had a bad experience in the past. Even when clients trust you, they may view the information you request as too personal or inappropriate. In some African cultures writing down a medical case history is not customary (16). Those clients may feel uneasy about your use of such information and, therefore, be unwilling to discuss their past. Also, in some cultures where only the doctor has medical authority, clients may be unwilling to provide health information to others. Be aware that in the United States public polls, surveys, and interviews have conditioned us to freely provide information to strangers; however, this is not common practice in many countries.

Your personal characteristics such as your age, sex, educational level, or ethnicity may influence the accuracy of your client's response. Some groups, for example, may not be comfortable giving certain information to a counselor of the opposite sex, particularly in the situation of a male client from a patriarchal culture with a female counselor. Also, clients may tell only what they think you want to hear in an effort to please or appear acculturated to the "American way." When an interpreter is used, those same barriers can alter the information being translated.

Suggested Approaches

- Establish rapport and show a genuine concern for the client. This will build a level of trust that encourages more accurate responses.

- Ask questions in several different ways to cross-check on the information obtained.

- Adjust the style of interaction to complement differences in age between you and the client. If you are younger, try to adopt a more serious and respectful attitude toward elderly clients. Conversely, if you are older, you may need to make special efforts to create an informal atmosphere that allows young clients to open up and speak freely.

- Use open-ended questions rather than questions requiring only "yes" or "no" responses; this may increase the amount of information you obtain.

Quick Guide for Cross-Cultural Counseling

Preparing for Counseling

- Understand your own cultural values and biases.

- Acquire basic knowledge of cultural values, health beliefs, and nutrition practices for client groups you routinely serve.

- Be respectful of, interested in, and understanding of other cultures without being judgmental.

Enhancing Communication

- Determine the level of fluency in English and arrange for an interpreter, if needed.

- Ask how the client prefers to be addressed.

- Allow the client to choose seating for comfortable personal space and eye contact.

- Avoid body language that may be offensive or misunderstood.

- Speak directly to the client, whether an interpreter is present or not.

- Choose a speech rate and style that promotes understanding and demonstrates respect for the client.

- Avoid slang, technical jargon, and complex sentences.

- Use open-ended questions or questions phrased in several ways to obtain information.

- Determine the client's reading ability before using written materials in the process.

Promoting Positive Change

- Build on cultural practices, reinforcing those which are positive, and promotin change only in those which are harmful.

- Check for client understanding and acceptance of recommendations.

- Remember that not all seeds of knowledge fall into a fertile environment to produce change. Of those that do, some will take years to germinate. Be patient and provide counseling in a culturally appropriate environment to promote positive health behavior.

References

1. Kohls, L.R., "The Values Americans Live By." Washington, D.C.: Meridian House International, 1984.

2. Watkins, E.L., and Johnson, A.E., ed. *Removing Cultural and Ethnic Barriers To Health Care, Proceedings of a National Conference.* Chapel Hill, North Carolina: University of North Carolina, 1979.

3. Orque, M.S., et. al., *Ethnic Nursing Care—A Multicultural Approach.* St. Louis, Missouri: C.V. Mosby Company, 1983.

4. Harwood, A., *Ethnicity and Medical Care.* Cambridge, Massachusetts: Harvard University Press, 1981.

5. *Cultural Diversity and Nursing Practice.* Irvine, California: Concept Media, Inc., 1979.

6. Bryant, Carol A., et al., *The Cultural Feast: An Introduction to Food and Society.* St. Paul, Minnesota: West Publishing Company, 1985.

7. Henderson, G., et al., *Transcultural Health Care.* Menlo Park, California: Addison-Wesley Publishing Company, 1981.

8. Wong, C. "Yin and Yang of Nutrition." *Perinatal Nutrition Newsletter* p. 1, California Department of Health Services, April-June, 1985.

9. Snow, L.F., and Johnson, S.M., "Folklore, Food, Female Reproductive Cycle." *Ecology of Food and Nutrition* 7:47-49, 1978.

10. U.S. Department of Health and Human Services, *Report of the Surgeon General's Workshop on Breastfeeding and Human Lactation.* Washington, D.C.: U.S. Government Printing Office, 1984.

11. Clark, A.L., *Culture, Childbearing, Health Professionals.* Philadelphia, Pennsylvania: F.A. Davis, 1978.

12. Clark, A.L., *Culture and Childrearing.* Philadelphia, Pennsylvania: F.A. Davis Company, 1981.

13. Kohls, L.R., Executive Director, The Washington International Center. Personal Communication, Washington, D.C., 1985.

14. Ramsey, S.J., "Nonverbal Behavior: An Intercultural Perspective," in Asante, M.K., et al., *Handbook of Intercultural Communication,* pp. 104-137. Beverly Hills, California: Sage Publications, 1979.

15. Range, M., Consultant, School for International Training. Personal Communication, Washington, D.C., 1985.

16. *Culture-Bound and Sensory Barriers to Communication with Patients: Strategies and Resources for Health Education.* Division of Health Education, Center for Health Promotion and Education, Centers for Disease Control, Atlanta, Georgia, 1982.

17. Dillard, J.M., *Multicultural Counseling.* Chicago, Illinois: Nelson-Hall, 1983.

Selected Bibliography

Cross-Cultural Communication

Asante, M.R., et al., ed, *Handbook of Intercultural Communication.* Beverly Hills, California: Sage Publications, 1979.

Atkinson, D., et al., *Counseling American Minorities.* Dubuque, Iowa: William C. Brown Co., 1979.

Casse, P., *Training for the Cross-Cultural Mind - A Handbook for Cross-Cultural Trainers and Consultants.* Washington, D.C.: Society for Intercultural Education, Training and Research, 1981.

Casse, P., *Training for the Multicultural Manager.* Washington, D.C.: Society for Intercultural Education, Training and Research, 1982.

Culture-Bound and Sensory Barriers to Communication With Patients: Strategies and Resources for Health Education. Division of Health Education, Center for Health Promotion and Education, Centers For Disease Control, Atlanta, Georgia, 1982.

Danish, S.J., et al., *Helping Skills: A Basic Training Program.* New York: Behavioral Publications, 1973.

Dillard, J.M., *Multicultural Counseling.* Chicago, Illinois: Nelson-Hall, 1983.

Kohls, L.R., *Developing Intercultural Awareness.* Washington, D.C.: Society for Intercultural Education, Training and Research, 1981.

Pederson, P.B., et al., ed, *Counseling Across Cultures.* Honolulu, Hawaii: University Press of Hawaii, 1976.

Putsch, R.W., "Cross-Cultural Communication—The Special Case of Interpreters in Health Care." *JAMA* 254(23): 3344-3348, 1985.

Stewart, E.C., *American Cultural Patterns - A Cross-Cultural Perspective.* Yarmouth, Maine: Intercultural Press, Inc., 1972.

Cultural Influences on Health and Nutrition

Bartholomew, M.J., and Poston, F.E., "Effect on Food Taboos on Prenatal Nutrition." *Journal of Nutrition Education,* 2:15-17, 1970.

Brink, P.J., ed., *Transcultural Nursing—A Book of Readings.* Englewood Cliffs, New Jersey: Prentice-Hall, Inc., 1976.

Brownlee, A.T., *Community, Culture and Care: A Cross-Cultural Guide for Health Workers.* St. Louis, Missouri: C.V. Mosby Company, 1978.

Brown, L.K., and Mussell, K., *Ethnic and Regional Foodways in the United States.* Knoxville, Tennessee: The University of Tennessee Press, 1984.

Bryant, C.A., et al., *The Cultural Feast—Introduction to Food and Society.* St. Paul, Minnesota: West Publishing Company, 1985.

Cassidy, C.M., "Subcultural Prenatal Diets of Americans," in *Alternative Dietary Practices and Nutritional Abuses in Pregnancy,* Proceedings of a Workshop, pp. 25-60. Washington, D.C.: National Academy Press, 1982.

Clark, A.L., *Culture, Childbearing, Health Professionals.* Philadelphia, Pennsylvania: F.A. Davis Company, 1978.

Clark, A.L., *Culture and Childrearing.* Philadelphia, Pennsylvania: F.A. Davis Company, 1981.

Cultural Diversity and Nursing Practice. Irvine, California: Concept Media, Inc., 1979.

Danford, D.E., "Pica and Nutrition." *Annual Reviews of Nutrition* 2:303-22, 1982.

"Ethnic, Social, and Economic Influences on Diet Patterns" in *Nutrition During Pregnancy and Lactation,* Chapter 8, pp. 75-93. California Department of Health, 1975.

Harwood, A., *Ethnicity and Medical Care.* Cambridge, Massachusetts: Harvard University Press, 1981.

"Healthy Mothers" Market Research: How to Reach Black and Mexican American Women. Office of Public Affairs, Public Health Service, U.S. Department of Health and Human Services, Washington, D.C., 1982.

Henderson, G., et al., *Transcultural Health Care.* Menlo Park, California: Addison-Wesley Publishing Company, 1981.

Hongladarom, G.C., and Russell, M., "An Ethnic Difference - Lactose Intolerance." *Nursing Outlook* 24:764-765, 1975.

Gifft, H.H., et al., *Nutrition, Behavior, and Change.* Englewood Cliffs, New Jersey: Prentice-Hall, Inc., 1972

Leininger, M., *Transcultural Nursing: Concepts, Theories, and Practices.* New York: John Wiley and Sons, 1978.

Litwach, L., et al., *Health Counseling.* New York: Appleton-Century-Crofts, 1980.

Orque, M.S., et al., *Ethnic Nursing Care—A Multicultural Approach.* St. Louis, Missouri: C.V. Mosby Company, 1983.

Sanjur, D., *Social and Cultural Perspectives in Nutrition.* Englewood Cliffs, New Jersey: Prentice-Hall, Inc., 1982.

Snow, L.F., and Johnson, S.M., "Folklore, Food, Female Reproductive Cycle." *Ecology of Food and Nutrition* 7:41-49, 1978.

Watkins, E.L., and Johnson, A.E., ed., *Removing Cultural and Ethnic Barriers to Health Care,* Proceedings of a National Conference. Chapel Hill, North Carolina: University of North Carolina, 1979.

Asian and Pacific Americans

A Guide to Orientation Materials for Indochinese Refugees and their Sponsors - A Selected Annotated Bibliography. Washington, D.C.: Center for Applied Linguistics, 1981.

Bulfer, J., et al., *Nutrition Education for Southeast Asians.* Minneapolis, Minnesota: Minneapolis Health Department, January 1981.

Chang, B., "Some Dietary Beliefs in Chinese Folk Culture." *Journal of the American Dietetic Association* 65(4): 436-8, 1974.

Health Workers' Guide To Indochinese Refugees. Edmonton, Alberta: Alberta Advanced Education and Manpower Settlement Services, 1980.

The Peoples and Cultures of Cambodia, Laos, and Vietnam. Washington, D.C.: Center for Applied Linguistics, 1981.

Tong, A., "Food Habits of Vietnamese Immigrants." *Family Economics Review* 2:28-30, 1986.

U.S. Department of Agriculture, Food and Nutrition Service, *Southeast Asian American Fact Sheets,* FNS-224 through FNS-230. U.S. Government Printing Office, Washington, D.C., September 1980.

Wong, C., "Yin and Yang of Nutrition." *Perinatal Nutritional Newsletter* p. 1, California Department of Health Services, April-June, 1985.

Yip, B.C., et al., *Understanding the Pan Asian Client.* San Diego, California: Union of Pan Asian Communities, 1978.

Black Americans

Blackwell, J., *The Black Community: Diversity and Unity.* New York: Dodd, Mead and Company, 1975.

Jerome, N.W., "Diet and Acculturation: The Case of Black American In-Migrants," in Jerome, N.W. et al., *Nutrition Anthropology.* Pleasantville, N.Y.: Redgrave Publishing, 1980.

Jones, D.L., "African-American Client, Clinical Practice Issues." *Social Work* 24:114, March 1979.

Kochman, T., *Black and White Styles in Conflict.* Chicago, Illinois: University of Chicago Press, 1981.

Luckraft, D.; *Black Awareness: Implications for Black Patient Care.* New York: American Journal of Nursing, 1976.

Norman, J.C., ed., *Medicine in the Ghetto.* New York: Appleton-Century-Crofts, 1969.

Snow, L., "Traditional Health Beliefs and Practices Among Lower Class Black Americans." *The Western Journal of Medicine.* p.p. 820-828, December 1983.

Hispanic Americans   Bailey, M.A., "Nutrition Education and the Spanish-Speaking American." *Journal of Nutrition Education* 2:50-54, Fall 1970.

Cardenos, J., et al., "Nutritional Beliefs and Practices in Primigravid Mexican-American Women." *Journal of the American Dietetic Association.* 69:262-265, 1976.

Crane, N. T., "Nutritional Status of Hispanic Americans." *Public Health Currents* 23(5), September-October 1983.

Hunt, I.F., et al., "Protective Foods Recall As a Tool for Dietary Assessment in the Evaluation of Public Health Programs for Pregnant Hispanics." *Ecology of Food and Nutrition* 12:235-245, 1983.

Martinez, R.A., *Hispanic Culture and Health Care: Fact, Fiction, Folklore.* St. Louis Missouri: C.V. Mosby Company, 1978.

Quesada, G.M., "Language and Communication Barriers for Health Delivery to a Minority Group." *Social Science and Medicine* 10:323-327, 1976.

Native Americans   Butte, N.F., et al., "Nutrition Assessment of Pregnant and Lactating Navajo Women." *American Journal of Clinical Nutrition* 34:2216-2228, 1981.

Niethammer, C., *American Indian Food and Lore.* New York: MacMillan Publishing Company, Inc., 1974.

Nutrition, Growth and Development of North American Indian Children, HEW Publication No. (NIH) 72:26. U.S. Government Printing Office, Washington, D.C., 1972.

Primeaux, M., "American Indian Health Care Practices: A Cross-Cultural Perspective." *Nursing Clinics of North America* 12(1):55-65, March 1977.

Primeaux, M., "Caring for the American Indian Patient." *American Journal of Nursing* January, 1977, p. 91.

Read, M.H., and Boling, M.A., "Effect of Feeding Practices on the Incidence of Iron Deficiency Anemia and Obesity in a Native American Population." *Nutrition Reports International* 26:689-694, 1984.

U.S. Department of Agriculture, Food and Nutrition Service, *Nutrition Education for Native Americans: A Guide for Nutrition Educators,* FNS-249. U.S. Government Printing Office, Washington, D.C., September 1984.

U.S. Department of Interior, Bureau of Indian Affairs, *Information About Indians,* 1978.

Appendix

A Brief Look at Four Cultural Minority Groups:
Relevant Sociocultural Issues*

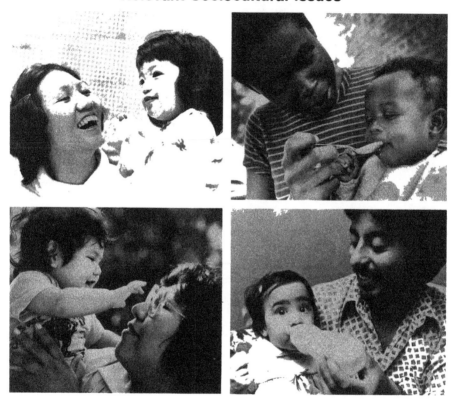

*Adapted from *Culture-Bound and Sensory Barriers to Communication With Patients: Strategies and Resources for Health Education,* Division of Health Education, Centers For Disease Control, Center for Health Promotion and Education CDC Contract No. 200-79-0916, August 1982, and "Subcultural Prenatal Diets of Americans," by Claire M. Cassidy in *Alternative Dietary Practices and Nutritional Abuses in Pregnancy,* National Research Council, 1982.

Asian and
Pacific Americans

Among Asian and Pacific Americans are included those cultural groups that have migrated from China, Japan, Korea, and Southeast Asia, as well as Hawaii, Philippines, Samoa, and Guam. Three general categories of Asian Americans have been identified. They represent varying degrees of acculturation and assimilation into Anglo-American culture related, to a great extent, to age at time of immigration and length of residence in the United States. Specific behavioral characteristics distinguish the three categories:

- Those who maintain traditional Asian values and behavior, which include obedience to parents, respect for authority, self-control of strong feelings, humility, praise of others, and blame of self for failure; health- and illness-related practices manifest a balancing of Asian and Western traditions.

- Those who practice both traditional Asian and Western values and behaviors, which include a degree of respect for parents and authority, individual self-assertiveness, lack of self-effacement, and some expression of feelings. Health- and illness-related practices are predominantly Western, but maintain some Asian characteristics. They are likely to be either immigrants who have been acculturated to some extent or U.S.-born children of immigrants who have been exposed to both cultures.

- Those who have fully adopted Western values and behavior, which include development of individuality, openness of expression, assertiveness, independence, and self-confidence. Health- and illness-related practices approach those of middle-class Americans. This group is likely to be U.S.-born Asian Americans whose parents or grandparents may also be U.S. born.

New immigrants generally would fall into the first category. However, it is important to stress that these characteristics vary in degree according to individuals and groups, and only some of these may be present in any one culture.

Family Relationships. Family structure varies in Asian cultures. It is useful for practitioners to know whether a client is from an extended or nuclear family in order to better identify resources which are appropriate to the client in terms of family involvement in the health care/treatment process. Authority of the household can rest with either the father, the mother, or both. This has implications for decision-making in terms of health care, and the counselor should consult with the appropriate authority of the household when major decisions are to be made. For example, authority may rest with the father-mother pair, or decisions may be made by the father alone. In most of the cultures, a husband often will act as a spokesperson for his wife.

Medical Beliefs and Practices. Asian and Pacific cultures are characterized by the Yin-Yang philosophy. Yin and Yang represent opposites of each other, but are complementary in nature. A hot-cold classification of foods as well as diseases are generally categorized according to the balance of Yin and Yang, although specific classification of foods and/or diseases varies according to the particular culture. Yin diseases fall into a cold category, while Yang diseases are considered hot. For example, cancer is representative of Yin, a cold disease, whereas an ear infection is thought of as a hot disease, or Yang. Yin illnesses would be treated by Yang foods, and Yang illnesses would be treated by Yin foods.

Dietary Practices. Oriental food traditions are ancient and complex. Diet is intimately associated with health, and in a complex manner with the condition of the cosmos. Of all cultures the diets of Chinese are perhaps the most intimately linked philosophically to all other aspects of its society, although this is also true for other Oriental peoples, for Hindus, and for other adherents to hot-cold theories of health.

Oriental cookery is characterized by mixed dishes with the components cut into small pieces; preparation is lengthy, but cooking time is often brief. Characteristic foods include rice and wheat, pork, chicken, a variety of vegetables (served barely cooked), eggs, various soy preparations, and tea. A favorite sauce combines sweet and sour flavors. Salt intake is high, fat low. Milk use is rare, and adult lactase deficiency is virtually universal.

A study of Vietnamese refugees in Florida indicated retention of a strong preference for Vietnamese foods after 4 years' residence in the United States. Vietnamese diets emphasize fish, rice, fresh vegetables, and tea. In the United States, use of such items as milk, beef, butter, eggs, potatoes, candy, fruit, and carbonated beverages rose. However, the only American food well liked was steak, and active dislike was widely expressed for such American standard choices as breakfast cereal, sandwiches, cake, pizza, and hamburgers. Consumption of carbonated beverages was quite high.

Black Americans

The sociohistorical relationship between Black Americans and Anglo-Americans has left broad gaps in levels of trust and communication. Cultural differences, access to services, poverty, and level of education are only some of the barriers to effective medical treatment and health education. Sensitivity to some of these issues depends in part on understanding some basic sociocultural characteristics that influence health practices by Black Americans.

For example, adverse environmental and economic factors can increase stress and lead to poor health. Many Black Americans live in conditions of poverty that prevent their access to and utilization of conventional health care. It is important to recognize that many of these factors are caused by barriers to socioeconomic mobility. An awareness of the socioeconomic issues that affect minorities can assist the counselor in being sensitive to the needs of the client in terms of both physical and emotional support. In addition, counselors should be informed about the common diseases more prevalent in the Black population.

Family Relationships. Black American culture is influenced in part by African heritage. The extended family and interdependent kinship ties are characteristic of both rural and urban communities. Health care is often viewed as a family responsibility, not just that of the individual and health care provider. The provider therefore can often solicit other family members as aides in caring for an ill Black American. Interdependence and interchangeability of roles within a family setting are often present in Black American families. Therefore, decision-making within the family may rest with either a male or female as head of the household.

Religious Beliefs. Because religion is an important aspect in Black American culture, members of the clergy are an integral part of the Black community. In many communities, they are trusted by and familiar with family members to such a degree that they can be helpful to counselors as liaisons between a family and a health practitioner or institution.

Because religion is such an integral part of the culture, illness may be viewed as punishment by God for sins. Therefore, the counselor should be alerted that feelings of guilt may be influential in the client's perception of an illness. In such instances, the counselor may want to consult with, or suggest that the client meet with, a member of the clergy in addition to health care providers. In some instances, religious beliefs and practices have been perceived as mental illness; for example, a client may report hearing or talking with God. This, however, might just be an expression of a client's religious belief.

Much of Black folk medicine comprises elements from both Christian and traditional African tribal religions. Traditional healing practices include mystic (supernatural) phenomena, psychological support, and herbal remedies. Herbal practices are found in rural and urban areas. In urban centers, religious and folk medicine practitioners provide psychological and spiritual support.

In urban areas, Black spiritual advisors and folk medicine practitioners are often called on to relieve anxieties and fears. In this way, they perform the role of psychotherapists. Charms and other objects may be worn for protection or as a form of preventive medicine. For example, a small bag containing herbs or other elements may be worn to ward off evil spirits.

Clients who express belief in witchcraft should be taken seriously. It is helpful for the counselor to find out why the client feels she or he has been a victim of witchcraft, because this information can help the provider make a determination for diagnosis or treatment of an illness. Black clients may be reluctant to talk about witchcraft or folk practices they have utilized. However, in order to provide appropriate treatment, it is important for the health care provider to ask specifically which healing practices have been used in order to determine openness to conventional health care.

Communication. The dialect used by some Black Americans is an integral part of Black American culture. It has been influenced by English and African languages as well as by geographical location and social factors. The health terminology used by the counselor can be confusing or misunderstood by a client even though she or he speaks English. It is important for counselors to speak clearly and to explain terminology when discussing matters concerning medical treatment. A familiarity with lay medical terminology and its differences from scientific terminology can help avoid misunderstandings in communication and misinterpretation of symptoms the client describes. It also is important for the counselor not to try to adopt Black English unnaturally, because this may be viewed by a Black client as both patronizing and inappropriate.

Dietary Practices. It is somewhat artificial to separate Black Americans from Anglo-Americans in describing diet, for Black Americans typically consume a regional cookery that does not differ much from those used by their Anglo neighbors. Several factors, however, make it worthwhile to discuss Black Americans' diet separately. First, there are more low-income Blacks, and low incomes are associated with less nutritious diets. Second, many Black Americans are lactose intolerant; therefore, their consumption of dairy foods is lower and reports of disliking and avoiding milk are frequent. Thus, designing a diet adequate in calcium requires special attention for counselors working with pregnant Black women. Finally, several dietary practices are widely used by Black Americans in selecting their diets. These have important nutritional implications.

Southern diets are distinguishable because they contain more corn, rice, pork, lard, legumes, and greens than do northern ones. Hot breads and fried foods are popular. An analysis of nutritional adequacy in 250 low-income Black homes in Misissippi showed mean intakes of protein, vitamin A, thiamin, riboflavin, and ascorbic acid to be above the 1974 Recommended Dietary Allowances, while mean intakes of energy, calcium, iron, and preformed niacin were below allowances. Only calcium was judged inadequate. Adolescents had the least nutritious diets; adult women had superior intakes except for calcium and iron.

While one study found that southern Black families of all income groups use less milk and fewer milk products than do white families, another study found that New York State Blacks consume nearly as much milk as do New York State Anglos. This could be interpreted as a strong cultural influence overriding lactose intolerance.

One analysis of dietary changes in Black families moving from the South to the North revealed that the noon meal was the first to change toward a northern pattern (i.e., sandwich, soup, fruit). Noncitrus fruit juices were preferred and were used as snack foods. More beef, potatoes, citrus, and milk were consumed in the North and less pork, chicken, lard, cornmeal, sugar, greens, and legumes.

Important food beliefs that affect food selection among Black Americans are shared by many Anglos. Foods may be classified as "heavy" (cornbread, greens, legumes) or "light" (fruit, white bread). A balanced meal consists of a mixture of heavy and light foods. Also, some foods are "strength" foods, e.g., vegetables, meat, and milk. Note the contrast with the middle-class American diet, which would interpret meat as more strengthening than vegetables.

An important belief has to do with the quality and character of the blood. A healthy body displays a balance of hot and cold (humors). Blood is hot. "High blood" (excess blood in the body) can cause stroke and is believed to come from eating too much rich food or red meat, such as pork. The treatment is believed to be dietary: use astringent and acidic foods, such a vinegar, lemons, pickles, or epsom salts to "open the pores and let the excess be sweated out." These ideas are important to the prenatal diet because the pregnant woman is "hot." She must control her diet to protect herself from "high blood," and this may involve avoiding meats and high-caloric foods or increasing the intake of sodium-rich foods. Additionally, the term "high blood" is confused with high blood pressure, so that individuals holding this misconception who are told their blood pressure is high may ingest items with a high sodium content as a form of self-treatment or eliminate meat from a diet which may already be protein-deficient.

One may also suffer from "low blood," which is equated with less blood in the body. In this case the dietary treatment is believed to be increased intake of liver, beets, rare meat, or milk. Note the emphasis on the color red and the bloodiness of the meat. The term "low blood" is sometimes confused with anemia, but in this case biomedical treatments and lay treatment may coincide. However, the treatment of low blood does conflict with the fairly widespread belief that pregnant women should not be exposed to blood. Some associate exposure to blood in pregnancy with danger of miscarriage. This is, perhaps, a good case for iron supplementation.

The ideas about blood, shared by many Black Americans and Anglo-Americans, derive from the Greek humoral theory, which remained the basis of conventional American medical practice well into the 19th century. Note that blood disorders are treated by dietary manipulation. Thus, to this extent, food is a medicine.

A final health habit that has dietary implications for the pregnant woman is the regular use of laxatives, which is practiced in many Black communities. The purpose is to remove impurities that come from eating an improper diet; this idea is also common among low-income Anglos.

Hispanic Americans

Hispanics constitute the second largest ethnic minority group in the United States. Generally, the following groups are referred to as Hispanics: Cubans, Mexican Americans or Chicanos, Mexican immigrants, Puerto Ricans, and South Americans. It must be emphasized that Hispanic cultures are diverse with important cultural differences existing among these groups. Many of these differences are a result of extremely varied historical, social, economic, and political experiences.

Family Relationships. Identification with and unity of the family are highly valued and constitute the nucleus of Hispanic culture. Close kinship relationships characterize the family structure, which is a primary source of emotional, physical, and psychological support. Family structure may be either extended or nuclear. The nuclear family is comprised of immediate members, i.e., father, mother, and children. The extended family incorporates other relatives, such as the grandparents, aunts, uncles, and cousins.

Generally, authority in the Hispanic family rests with the eldest male. Most major decisions, therefore, will be made by either the father or the husband. In terms of health care, responsibility for care of an ill family member will rest with other family members. Usually, clients will have consulted with various family members before seeking outside care.

The Importance of Privacy. Modesty is highly valued. Health care professionals should take care to minimize situations in which a Hispanic client may feel compromised. In particular, communication between client and counselor should demonstrate respect for the client's needs in this area. Sensitivity to these cultural norms will help avoid embarrassment for parents and children. Interruptions of privacy during the consultation should always be avoided.

Religious Attitudes and Beliefs. Religious and fatalistic attitudes may influence a client's approach to an illness and its treatment. For example, the client may believe that illness is a result of punishment from God and that medical care cannot change the course or outcome of an illness. This has implications for the methods used for treatment as well as appropriate ways of communicating with the client about regimens. In terms of treatment, it is important to discuss what the

31

client's reservations are and to identify what steps the client might be willing to take. Second, it may be useful to refer the client to a respected member of her or his religion, e.g., a priest, to discuss how management of a medical problem fits within the religion's framework.

Folk medical beliefs, folk medical practitioners, and rituals comprise traditional Hispanic health practices. The hot-cold theory of disease organizes illnesses and cures into categories identified as either hot or cold. However, hot-cold categories vary among Hispanic groups. For example, Puerto Ricans have a "warm" classification in addition to hot and cold. Foods and herbs, as well as illnesses, are also classified in these categories. Unless the prescribed regimen fits the client's assessment of what treatment is appropriate, adherence to a regimen is likely to be minimal. Therefore, it is important for a counselor to identify the client's hypotheses about health problems and their treatment.

The *espiritista* (spiritualist) and/or *curandero* are some of the folk practitioners consulted when treatment is needed in many traditional Hispanic communities. They may be consulted before a conventional health practitioner. The counselor should ask the client whether he or she has consulted a folk practitioner and determine what folk remedies have been used.

One frequent reason for Hispanic clients' preference for traditional folk practitioners is distrust of conventional medicine and health care providers. Other factors in underutilization of conventional medical care are inadequate income, low level of education, and advanced age.

Communication. Communicating in English may be awkward or difficult for the client. It may change the client's expression of symptoms or may be misinterpreted. When language differences between Spanish-speaking clients and non-Spanish-speaking counselors exist, it is recommended that a bilingual interpreter be used. This may be a family member, a friend of the client, or a trusted individual within the community known by the client who is able to act as a liaison.

Dietary Practices. Mexican American and Puerto Rican diets differ, but food selection based on the hot-cold theory of health is shared by many in both subcultures.

The staples of Mexican American diets feature beans and tortillas made from corn treated with lime (calcium carbonate). Other popular foods are eggs, chicken, lard, chili peppers, onions, tomatoes, many varieties of squash, herb teas (mint, chamomile), sweetened packaged breakfast cereals, potatoes, bread, carbonated beverages, canned fruits, gelatin, ice cream, other sweets, and sugar. Milk is used mostly in hot beverages. Breakfast is often a very generous meal.

The following dishes are favorites in the Southwest: chili, chili con carne, enchiladas, tamales, tostadas, chicken mole, and nopalitos. Among Mexican American migrant workers in California, favorite dishes include refried beans, tacos, tortillas, and, to a lesser extent, such middle-class American dishes as hamburgers, macaroni and cheese, and hotdogs. Compared with Anglos, Mexican Americans used more carbonated beverages, beer, and sweetened beverage mixes, and less milk, coffee, and tea.

Mexican American diets are generally adequate for protein and energy but low for vitamin A, iron, and calcium. Obesity and anemia are common; pica is infrequent.

Puerto Rico diets feature beans and rice as the staple. Other popular foods include various meats, cornmeal, yams, sweet potatoes, onions, beets, eggplant, green peppers, tomatoes, lard, olive oil, pineapple, bananas, and sugar. Coffee with milk and custards serve as the main vehicles for milk.

Mexican American and Puerto Rican dietary practices also utilize the hot-cold system. In this system, foods have inherent (symbolic) temperatures, such as cold, neutral, or hot. A good meal provides a balance, and a person can get sick by eating foods whose temperature are wrong for him or her. A pregnant woman is "hot"—hence she must avoid both very hot and very cold foods. In practice this means that some pregnant Mexican American or Puerto Rican women will avoid chili peppers and some salty, fatty, or sweet foods ("hot") and acidic, sour, or fresh foods ("cold"); such as lemons, tomatoes, or watermelon. Unless these have formed an inordinate part of the prepregnancy diet, avoidance during pregnancy should have no unusually deleterious effects.

Medications, too, have inherent temperatures and a pregnant woman may refuse to take "hot" prescriptions. Iron supplements were defined as "hot" by some Puerto Rican clients in New York City. On the other hand, a sample of pregnant southwestern Mexican Americans regularly saw a doctor and took prescribed vitamins and minerals faithfully. Similarly, a sample of New England Puerto Ricans sought prenatal care and were quite compliant.

Native Americans

Broad differences exist among the many subcultures of Native Americans. It is therefore extremely important for the counselor to be aware of the cultural characteristics unique to the specific group and individual for whom they provide counseling. Presented here are some notes from the literature on Native American culture and health care. To help further identify these differences, health professionals may seek information about specific groups with whom they work by consulting their area's Indian Community Tribal Council or Indian health professionals.

As an example of the kinds of information that are available from such sources, the South Dakota United Indian Association provides information on cultural differences and has written a sensitivity packet for non-Indian health care providers. In one of its publications, the association describes the different lifestyles of traditional (reservation), contemporary (urban and reservation), and cosmopolitan Native Americans.

Traditional Native Americans maintain their culture and traditions within their communities through medicine men and religious practices. Their language and cultural practices are totally integrated into their daily activities. In comparison, the contemporary or bicultural Native American is usually found in urban centers. Some individuals are successful in becoming bicultural, while others are unable to cope with the "double standard" and exhibit mental and emotional instabilities, alcoholism, and drug abuse. Cosmopolitan Native Americans are integrated into

Anglo culture, often intermarry with Anglos, and adopt Anglo identities. Currently, however, a growing number of cosmopolitan Native Americans are returning to their tribal identity.

The persistence of traditional healing practices is an important factor in Native American health care. Due to the coexistence of traditional and conventional health care systems, there is a need to collaborate whenever possible with traditional health care practitioners.

Some Cultural Characteristics. Although the definition of immediate family members will differ among tribes, the Indian family structure is characterized by an extended family unit with strong kinship ties. Both matriarchal and patriarchal systems function in certain tribes with ownership passed on through the mother, and also communal, i.e., shared with others. Interdependency between individuals and responsibility to the tribe are highly valued, as are respect for an individual's rights and noninterference in another's personal life unless requested. Respect for elders is also a primary element of Native American culture.

A number of cultural characteristics of Native Americans may have a marked impact on the success of communication with and treatment of clients from this cultural group. For example, closeness to nature is characteristic of Native American cultures, and death is accepted as a part of the natural cycle. The concept of time is based on a continuum that focuses on the present rather than the future. There is a strong belief that many events cannot be altered by humans.

Religious Beliefs and **Tribal Healing Practices.** Religion helps to maintain stability and gives a sense of cohesion to an individual's life; it is not separated from health care as it is in most Western cultures. The religion is based on belief in the almighty Mother Earth. "Bad" happenings are viewed as punishment, and "good" happenings viewed as reward. Religion is incorporated into daily activities and maintained by teaching and example. Religious and healing practices are interrelated in rituals, and illness is interpreted as a sign of disharmony with nature. Native Americans have a holistic concept of health care. Signs, symptoms, as well as causes are treated. Illness is considered to be caused by either natural or supernatual influences. Tribal rituals often involve the use of foods sacred to the particular tribe; for example, corn is considered curative by some groups. Cedar also may be important in religious healing rituals or in medicine bags.

Death rituals and taboos vary between groups, and attitudes vary about touching the body. Although tribal healing practices differ between groups they usually include:

— purification of the patient and the medicine man
— the Navajo practice of a Sign (ritual, chants, and sand painting lasting for various lengths of time)
— smoking religious tobacco
— gentle massage
— small sacrifices
— prayers

Other traditional approaches to health care are herbal remedies and bone setters. Some Indian groups take traditional medications, such as herbal teas, in large doses. Non-Indian medical care providers must be aware of the need to emphasize strongly the taking of prescribed medications according to directions.

Communication. Display of emotion is encouraged in some tribes but discouraged by others. Intense eye contact often is considered disrespectful; counselors have often misinterpreted this as the client being inattentive or disinterested. Handshakes are an important symbolic gesture, although in some groups a vigorous handshake is sometimes viewed as a sign of aggressiveness.

Many Native Americans do not speak English; among these are the many rural elderly who live on reservations. When an interpreter is needed a bilingual family member may be the most helpful person. Because public education is conducted primarily in English, children or grandchildren of elderly Native Americans in rural areas often are bilingual. However, misinterpretation can occur even with an interpreter. Some English words and concepts do not exist in Indian languages or are not easily translatable; the reverse is also true of some Indian words and concepts. Special care should be given to identify clearly the client's symptoms and to explain the illness. This requires more time and patience for both parties. If possible, counselors should meet with the interpreter before seeing the client in order to discuss more fully the best ways to communicate medical terms and treatment.

Dietary Practices. Dietary practices of Native Americans vary from region to region, according to the natural food supply of the area. The contemporary Native American diet combines indigenous natural foods with modern processed foods. Game and fish, where plentiful, provide important food sources. Fruits, berries, roots, and wild greens are highly valued foods, but scarce in many areas. When indigenous foods are not available, the daily diet consists of commodity foods donated by the U.S. Department of Agriculture and foods purchased at stores. In particular, fresh fruits and vegetables might not always be available for purchase or may be too expensive, unless locally grown.

Lack of refrigeration may greatly limit some Native Americans' consumption of fresh meat, milk, fruits, and vegetables. They must turn to nonperishable foods for the bulk of their diet. Consequently, their diets may lack variety and be marginal or deficient in key nutrients, but may be high in refined sugar, cholesterol, fat, and calories.

There are many culturally related food concepts which determine food acceptance. Among Navajo, meat and blue cornmeal are considered "strong" foods while milk is an example of a "weak" food. Corn is a sacred food to many Native American tribes and is used in ceremonies, such as weddings. Dietary taboos against many foods exist among different tribes. For example, some Plains Indians place a taboo on fish.

Evaluation Questionnaire

Dear Reader:

Please take a few minutes to answer some questions about this new publication. Your response will help us to evaluate and revise the guide. Once you have completed the questionnaire please fold it, seal with tape, and mail. Thank You!

Are you a Nutritionist_____Nurse_____Other (specify)_____

Do you work for WIC/CSFP_____health agency_____
other (specify)_____

Which State do you work in?

What cultural groups do you serve?

Anglo-Americans_____   Hispanic Americans_____
Asian and Pacific Americans_____   Native Americans_____
Black Americans_____   Other (specify)_____

Please comment on the content of the guide:

	Useful	Interesting but not useful	Other Comments
Overall Guide			
Understanding Section			
Communicating Section			
Bibliography			
Appendix			

Are you planning to use the guide?   _____ yes _____ no

Are you planning to share it with others?   _____ yes _____ no

If this publication was revised, what changes would you suggest?

Please list any resources and references you have found particularly useful in counseling clients from various cultural groups.

CPSIA information can be obtained
at www.ICGtesting.com
Printed in the USA
BVHW09*1114160818
524721BV00018B/2362/P